THROUGH THE L
UNIFORMS C
HOME GU

Above: Men of the Sussex (Rustington) L.D.V. on parade, July 1940. (By kind permission of Mrs. Mary Taylor)

RICHARD J. HUNT

To find out about other titles produced by Historic Military Press visit our website at www.historicmilitarypress.com.
Alternatively please write to us free of charge at: Customer Services, Historic Military Press, Freepost SEA 11014, Pulborough, West Sussex, RH20 4BR, or telephone our freephone number: 0800 071 7419.

HISTORIC MILITARY PRESS

UNIFORMS OF THE HOME GUARD

First published 2002 by Historic Military Press,
ISBN 1-901313-16-6

ACKNOWLEDGMENTS

This book would have not been possible without the following members of the 'Real Dad's Army' team. It was they who spent many an hour in Denim or Serge - not all of which was a best fit. My publishers also wish to express their gratitude to: Mick Barr; Richard Botting; Mike 'Bulldog' Carroll; Tony Dudman; Ralph De Straet Von Kollman; Christine Hunt; Mark Khan; Martin Mace; George Kimmins; Keith Major; Cliff Skinner and Dave Wickens. The following are also to be thanked for their permission to reproduce archive photographs: Mr. Kim Leslie and the West Sussex County Archivist; Mr. Stewart Angell; Mrs. Mary Taylor; The Kent Messenger; and The Sussex Express.

Front cover: A Private of the 21st Sussex (Eastbourne) Battalion Home Guard, 1941. He is pictured here on duty at Hope Gap, near Eastbourne, watching for the impending arrival of a German invasion fleet. He is in greatcoat order, with light equipment, and a P.17 Rifle and bayonet.

Printed in the United Kingdom by D.C. Data Systems, 95 Poulters Lane, Worthing, West Sussex, BN14 7SY. Tel: 01903 525695

HISTORIC MILITARY PRESS
Green Arbor, Rectory Road, Storrington, West Sussex, RH20 4EF. Telephone/Fax: 01903 741941

www.historicmilitarypress.com.

In recent times the interest in the British Home Front during the Second World War, and in particular that unique organisation the Home Guard, has increased tremendously. Such topics now figure prominently in the National Curriculum, as well as appearing on television, at the cinema and in literature. Equally, amateur historians, collectors and re-enactors enthusiastically acquire the memorabilia from this period.

It may be that all this has, in part, been due to a wave of nostalgia for times and attitudes that seem to be disappearing fast. Regular re-runs of the comedy series 'Dad's Army' has only served to retain the Home Guard in the memory of the British public and remind us a little of the situation and attitudes of that time - even if somewhat exaggerated for a comic effect. Many would fail to recognise that a number of the equipment and uniform details used within these programmes are inaccurate.

Aware of the confusing and sometimes apparently conflicting information on the uniforms and equipment of the L.D.V. and Home Guard presented in some books, it was decided that the time had come to present all the important details in a new, clear and concise manner. Now, in one book, and at an easy glance, the collector, historian, re-enactor and 'man in the street' can tell what would, most likely, be the correct appearance of an ordinary Home Guard or Local Defence Volunteer at any particular period of the war. It is hoped, therefore, that the various transitional stages of the Home Guard have been shown without the need to compose a monumental tome of learned but impossibly difficult to interpret facts.

Research has been helped by the wealth of photographic and cinematic material that was available. One main problem encountered was that many privately taken photographs were not specifically dated. Even eyewitness accounts are not always reliable for, after more than half a century, the memory can play frustrating tricks on an individual. Where possible, reference has been made to contemporary Army Council, L.D.V. or Home Guard instructions in an effort to provide the reader with accurate time lines.

It is important to stress that any allotment of weapons, uniform or equipment to the Home Guard was always dependant upon supply and availability. In general there was no simultaneous issue of kit to the entire Home Guard. Such matters could be decided by whoever was considered a tactical priority. Some inland units might wait many months for the likes of steel helmets and service respirators, whilst coastal battalions in Kent and Sussex may have been equipped very quickly.

This work has been compiled, with the help of the 'Real Dad's Army Historical Re-enactment Group', using original uniforms and equipment of the period all of which are preserved in private collections. It is hoped that these reconstructions will provide a valuable insight into an important aspect of Britain's most endearing wartime institution - the Home Guard.

It was on the 14th May 1940 that Anthony Eden made his famous broadcast on the BBC that led to the formation of, initially, the LDV, and ultimately the Home Guard. Some days later, on the 22nd May, Sir Edward Grigg, the then Under Secretary of State for War, made a speech in the House of Commons and elaborated further. Making some of the first references to uniforms and equipment, he announced that "uniforms will consist of linen overalls and field service caps, or civilian clothes with khaki armbands stitched to the sleeve, having the letters 'L.D.V.' stencilled on the armband in white. Volunteers wearing civilian clothes with armbands will be issued with field service caps".

The volunteer shown here is wearing his three-piece suit of mid-1930s style, with separate collared shirt, trilby hat and civilian shoes. He has the earliest officially produced black-on-white printed L.D.V. armband. These were issued over the few weeks following the initial call-to-arms. Due to the inability of the government to provide satisfactory quantities, mainly due to unexpected numbers of men volunteering, many areas resorted to locally producing armbands of varying types and quality. It was soon realised that white armbands were too conspicuous, and were in turn replaced by black-on-khaki varieties.

Initially, as with uniforms, there were no weapons available, and so for a while improvisation was to be the order of the day. Clubs, knives lashed to broom handles, pick helves, pitchforks and of course anything that could shoot was eagerly pressed into service. Shooting ranges, Cadet Corps and even museums were mercilessly plundered. Even if you could not fire it, you could certainly drill with it.

Everything from garden guns to fine quality sporting guns could be seen on parades across the nation. Many ex-army officers still retained their service revolvers and ammunition, in some cases dating as far back as the Boer War or beyond.

The volunteer here is carrying his civilian type gas mask in its original cardboard carrying case. He has armed himself with one of the first locally made petrol bombs used by the L.D.V., - the Molotov cocktail.

This postal worker, although fit and of an age to be called up, is exempt by virtue of being on the 1939 "Reserved Occupations" list. This states that Postal workers over the age of 35 were to be exempt from compulsory conscription. He is still in civilian clothes, but has advanced a stage in that he has been issued with an armband - in this case bearing the G.P.O. Battalion red unit stamps at either side of 'LDV'. At this stage many of the volunteer units were being formed around places of work, such as bus garages, factories, post offices and railway depots - even the Palace of Westminster had its own company.

A printed L.D.V. armband. This example carries an identification stamp with the wording "Hove Assembly Room."

He may well have attended the G.P.O. Signals School, which was in Brighton, where personnel received training in the use of the military wireless communication equipment of the period. He has his Universal Pattern Field Service Cap (cap badges were yet to be authorised), but best of all, he has a proper weapon. In this instance he has a British Army Short Magazine Lee Enfield .303 rifle, and more specifically a No.1 Mk.3*. Many L.D.V. units received initial stocks of these rifles, only to have them hastily reclaimed later. Desperately trying to reform and re-arm in the aftermath of the withdrawal from Dunkirk, where they were forced to abandon much of their equipment, the Military Authorities soon realised that the weapons initially supplied to the L.D.V. were needed by the Regular Army. Many other units received bulk issues of obsolete rifles such as Long Lee Enfields, some dating as far back as 1900.

He is still carrying his civilian issue respirator in its cardboard case, though it was soon found that these did not stand up to the rigours of military training. As a stopgap measure 'containers, tin, for civilian pattern respirators' were issued for use until service pattern respirators and bags eventually appeared.

A typical pair of black leather civilian shoes of the period. So called 'utility' shoes like these were the footwear of the L.D.V. and Home Guard until the issue of military 'ammunition boots', which did not appear for many months.

This was one of six battalions formed by the employees of Southern Railway for the defence and security of the South Coast railway network that stretched from Devon to Kent. Initiated on June 2nd 1940, some 18,000 railwaymen had volunteered within a period of one week.

Army Council Instructions dated 24th of June 1940 decreed that the issue of equipment to each L.D.V. volunteer should be: one suit of denim overalls; one service respirator; one steel helmet; one field dressing and one field service cap. Indeed, on May 22nd 1940, Sir Edward Grigg announced that already 90,000 sets of Denim overalls had been issued, along with 250,000 Field Service Caps, and that a similar number of armbands were on order.

Now better uniformed, our volunteer has a complete suit of khaki denim overalls. These were introduced for the regular army in 1939 to protect the serge battledress whilst carrying out dirty tasks. Initially these were the only uniforms available in sufficient numbers to outfit the new force. Even so, the issue was variable in speed and quantity, many units receiving insufficient denims and waiting as long as the following spring to complete the transition. Despite such sporadic activities, it was still considered a matter of some urgency to get the L.D.V. into some form of uniform. It was publicly reported that Hitler was threatening to treat volunteers in the L.D.V., and later the Home Guard, not as soldiers, but as 'guerrilla' troops and execute them summarily if captured. An added bonus was that the issue of uniforms would also provide a great boost to the men's morale.

Over the next six months or so the denims of some units were replaced, to add to the confusion, by serge battle dress uniforms. In such cases, each unit was instructed to retain a proportion of denims, (25% of them), for their original use - protecting serge battledress when doing such dirty tasks as heavy weapons handling and decontamination.

The only insignia worn on the denims was the khaki armband. At first these were printed with 'L.D.V.' in black - this in turn being technically obsolete by July 31st 1940. The volunteer illustrated here has the tape tied panel variation with Southern Railway unit stamp. This has been inscribed with his national identity number. In time, the 'Home Guard' black-on-khaki printed armbands replaced these when they were finally delivered. Many units, such as the 12th Staffordshire Home Guard, did not have their original L.D.V. examples replaced until mid-September 1940. After armbands were withdrawn from general use, denims were worn unadorned. Research has shown that the denim blouse was usually of the 'utility' design, and the trousers of the '1937' Pattern.

Underneath his uniform he would be wearing his civilian shirt and underwear - other ranks never received the collar-less khaki flannel shirts of the regular army. This man is fortunate in that his issue of black leather British Army issue 'ammunition' boots has arrived, though most units at this time could still be found wearing their own plain black civilian shoes.

A Volunteer of the Rustington, West Sussex, L.D.V. on patrol with his dog. Note that, like our reconstruction, he is also wearing a cotton bandolier for .300 U.S. ammunition. (By kind permission of Mrs. M. Taylor)

Detail of a Southern Railway L.D.V. armband. In some units, officers had their ranks denoted on their armbands by varying numbers of red stars above the lettering. The actual stamp marking reads 'Southern Railway General Manager'.

Soon after the formation of the L.D.V., a deal was struck with the U.S. Government resulting in the shipping to the U.K. of nearly 800,000 Enfield Pattern 1917 .300, 5-shot, bolt action rifles. These were to arrive complete with their bayonets and ammunition. The rifles had been kept stored in thick grease since 1919, and the initial allocation of rifles was, like that of the denims, rather haphazard. Many units were supplied with only small quantities and had to pass a rifle from man to man as they came, and went, off duty. This volunteer carries the ammunition for his P.17 rifle in a disposable cotton six-pocket bandolier courtesy of the U.S. Government. He has, however, managed to retain a 1908 Patt.

Details on the contractors label in the denim overall blouse.

small pack from somewhere - after all, a soldier needs something to keep his rations in!

It is worth noting that on the 13th October 1940, recruiting into the Home Guard was temporarily suspended. The shortage of equipment, including greatcoats and capes, had become too severe. The War Office though, was taking measures to rectify the situation. Orders had been placed for enough battledress for every man: rubber knee-boots; torches and of course capes. Procurement of woollen gloves; mess-tins; water bottles; and one million tin containers for the civilian gas masks had also been set in motion.

EQUIPMENT LIST:
- **Field Service Cap**
- **Overalls, Denim Blouse**
- **Overalls, Denim Trousers**
- **Cotton bandolier for .300 U.S. ammunition**
- **Printed L.D.V. armband**
  - **1903 Patt. leather waist belt**
    - **P.17 .300 Enfield rifle with U.S. Army T.S.M.G. sling**
    - **British Army 1908 Patt. small pack and cross strap**
    - **Ammunition boots**

Thanks to the then Prime Minister, Winston Churchill, the name of the L.D.V. was changed on July 23rd 1940. The term 'Home Guard' was then officially adopted. Although serge uniform had started to be introduced from the autumn of 1940, a great many units did not receive it until as late as early 1941. The 'Battledress Blouse, Serge', with its unlined collar, was introduced into the British Army during 1939, together with the matching 'Battledress Trousers, Serge'. In the Home Guard, this uniform was at first worn with the black-on-khaki drill printed armband. In this example, the reduced rectangular panel only has been directly stitched to the sleeve.

Cap badges of a local county regiment were finally authorised to be worn by the Home Guard on their Field Service Caps on August 3rd 1940. They were only issued on a 'supplies available' basis. In some instances certain units were allowed their own individual unit cap badges - such as the Upper Thames Patrol. In our example, the volunteer would have worn the badge of his regular county regiment - the Royal Sussex Regiment. Several months later, on May 7th 1941, Army Council Instruction 721 also permitted that a Home Guard unit may play the Regimental March of the county regiment whose cap badge it wore.

The anklets are uniquely Home Guard, and were issued in mid-brown grained chrome leather. Commonly they were stained black by the wearer. The waist-belt was from the 1903 Patt. Greatcoat equipment, whereas the bayonet is the one for the .303 Canadian Ross rifle. Respected for its accuracy, it was a clumsy weapon when used in action and was found to be easily jammed by dirt. It is also unusual in that it has its own integral belt frog. The gas mask is a standard military respirator in its Mk.VI bag - at last replacing the civilian type masks. He has also received a steel helmet.

The question of gas masks often proved troublesome, especially for those Home Guards who worked in a public service industry. For these men would have had three gas masks - one civilian gas mask in the standard cardboard box; one civilian 'duty' respirator, and eventually the standard military issue respirator. Army Council Instruction 413, (March 24th 1941), decreed that the civilian respirators would not be withdrawn on the issue of the Service Pattern item, but that it would be retained for use at times other than when military duty is performed. Indeed, it confirmed that a Home Guard could only carry the Service Respirator when on Home Guard duty. Further notes followed. On July 7th 1941, Army Council Instruction 1152 informed the Home Guard that on all occasions of a purely private nature, only the standard civilian pattern gas mask was to be carried and used.

EQUIPMENT LIST
• Mark 2. steel helmet • Battle Dress Blouse, Serge • Battle Dress Trousers, Serge • 1903 Patt. waist belt • Reduced armband • Leather anklets • Ross rifle bayonet and frog • Ammunition boots • Service Patt. respirator and Mk. VI. bag

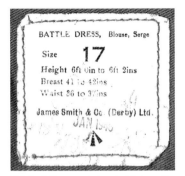

Detail of the manufacturer's label on the 'Battledress Blouse, Serge'.

With one of the Home Guard's watchwords being 'ingenuity', many sought to overcome shortages of official equipment by locally producing their own - such as this 'emergency' armband. (By kind permission of Mr. R. Botting)

Home Guard armband with red G.P.O. stamps. The G.P.O marking was introduced by the Post Office in conjunction with the War Office to provide an indication to Area Commanders, whose districts the G.P.O. units might be passing through, that they were engaged on a specific task of defending key communication points or maintaining essential defence circuits.

From the very beginning of the L.D.V. movement, mounted units were formed. It was seen that they would be able to cover a lot more ground in rural areas than the normal foot patrols. Reputedly, the first of these units was raised on Exmoor from the Devon and Somerset Staghounds and were known as the "Exmoor Mounties". Many counties rapidly followed suit, with many other local hunts forming mounted units - notable amongst which was the Devon Hunt, which may have had the unique distinction of forming a mounted ladies section. One unit formed at the very outset, in May 1940, was the mounted Home Guard unit that patrolled the North Yorkshire Moors. One of the original volunteers, Mr. N. Simpson, was photographed on August 8th 1940, whilst on patrol. Not only was he fully armed with P.17, he had the luxury of an almost complete uniform. His headgear took the form of a Khaki Service Dress Cap - though devoid of any Regimental badge.

Here, the mounted section of the Lewes Home Guard is shown. The Lewes area had strong racing connections, and it was considered that one of the best ways in which to patrol the open Sussex Downs around the town was on horseback. Amongst the all time high of 50 members, the unit sported the two brothers Richard and Bilby Rees. They had, respectively, won the Grand National in the years 1921 and 1922. The unit had appeared in a news film in 1941, and, through the interest generated locally, they became known as the "Lewes Cossacks".

Our volunteer is wearing the standard battle dress blouse with printed Home Guard armband with regular cavalry issue khaki Bedford cord pantaloons. At first equipped with leather riding boots or agricultural type gaiters, these were soon changed to long khaki puttees. A number of

Standard Home Guard printed black-on-khaki drill armband. On the reverse can be seen the stamp of the Somerset Territorial Army Association. It is certain that the 'Exmoor Mounties' would have been within the area controlled by the Somerset T.A. Association.

Left: An archive photograph of the 'Lewes Cossacks' or, more properly, the 16th Sussex, (Lewes), Home Guard. (By kind permission of the Sussex Express).

Home Guard mounted units wore khaki serge service dress peaked caps at various times. In the early days, they would have been armed with a double-barrelled 12-bore shotgun, possibly using buckshot rounds. This practice was soon changed to the same magazine rifles as the remainder of the parent battalion. Ammunition was carried in 5 or 9 pocket leather 1903 Patt. bandoliers and the standard 1903 Patt. waist belt was worn. By November 1943, the mounted units of the Home Guard were generally being phased out, replaced by more modern mechanised modes of transport. By this time, more than 40 counties nation-wide possessed mounted Home Guard units, employing some 900 horses.

EQUIPMENT LIST
- **Field Service Cap**
- **Battle Dress Blouse, Serge**
- **Pantaloons, Service Dress**
- **Khaki Serge puttees**
- **1903 Patt. cavalry bandolier**
- **1903 Patt. waist belt**
- **Home Guard printed armband**
- **Ammunition boots**

This Private is wearing Home Guard shoulder titles, officially authorised by War Office letter 54/H.G./36 of April 2nd 1941, but already unofficially acquired by many units. These were made in either printed buff-on-khaki drill, or buff embroidery on khaki serge. Printed county designations (regimental flashes) and battalion numbers were also authorised on this date. It seems that their supply was much later in coming, as many units wore the titles only for some considerable time.

Here the Home Guard is wearing a Short Magazine Lee Enfield bayonet in his 1939 Patt. leather belt frog. On his left hip he has the haversack of a design unique to the Home Guard. Introduced in 1940 it has an integral strap, the length of which could be modified by stitching in folds to reduce it. It was constructed of the rubberised material normally used for groundsheets and groundsheet capes.

On his right side is his water bottle. The cradle bears some similarities to the 1903 Patt. still being used by mounted troops as late as 1939, and was a type used only by the Home Guard or the Auxiliary Territorial Service. The canteen is the standard blue enamelled steel mark IV. model.

He is holding the legendary, and infamous, Home Guard pike. This was not a broomstick, or other home made weapon, but a government manufactured item made to strict design and measurements. Introduced well after the Home Guard had been properly equipped with a large variety of modern small arms and heavy support weapons, this was intended to be a close quarters weapon with which to engage the expected waves of enemy parachutists. It was received badly by the Home Guard who, by now, were becoming very conscious of the need for more effective equipment and more professional training. Many felt that appearing in public with such a bizarre and archaic weapon was somewhat demeaning to them. Indeed, questions were asked in the House of Commons about the waste of public funds, and materials, on these weapons.

British Army 'ammunition' boots. At the beginning of the war, these were fitted with 25 studs per boot, but as material shortages began to bite, this was reduced to 18, (Home Guard Information Circular No.5, November 8th 1941), and eventually just 13 per boot. Home Guard Information Circular No.4, published earlier on October 29th 1941, indicated that the local T.A. Association would be responsible for the repair of Home Guard boots. At the discretion of the local T.A. Commander, such repairs could be carried out locally in the town or village where a unit was located in an effort to keep costs and repair times to a minimum.

Men of the Rustington Home Guard on parade through their village. Issue of the Home Guard shoulder titles has started, but yet again the sporadic nature of such issues is evidenced by the fact that not all of the men have such titles on their battledress. (By kind permission of Mrs. M. Taylor)

EQUIPMENT LIST
• Field Service Cap • Battle Dress Blouse, Serge • Battle Dress Trouser, Serge • 1903 Patt. waistbelt • Home Guard special Pattern haversack • Mk. IV water bottle and H.G. Patt. cradle • Short Magazine Lee Enfield bayonet in 1939 Patt. frog • Home Guard pike • Leather anklets • Ammunition boots

Towards the end of 1941 the demand on the Regular Army to find men for overseas duties led to the War Office deciding that men from the Home Guard should be trained for use on certain defensive sites so that members of the Regular Army might be released.

In the summer of 1942, it was decided to use members of Home Guard Battalions to man some of the emergency Coastal Defence Batteries that were situated within their area. In doing so, this would release valuable members of the Royal Artillery. Not all Coastal Batteries were handed over to the Home Guard. The major peacetime forts, such as Fort Newhaven, were to remain under the control of the Regular Army. Others, such as those in weak strategic positions, would be placed onto a 'care-and-maintenance' basis only.

If we take West Sussex as an example, we know that the instructions for this transfer to Home Guard crews were issued in August 1942. Initially, the Royal Artillery was to be replaced at three emergency Coastal Batteries: at Worthing, by the 5th Sussex (Worthing) Home Guard; at Littlehampton, by the 6th (Arundel); and at Bognor Regis, by the 8th Sussex (Bognor and Selsey) Home Guard. Each Battery was to have an establishment of 2 Officers and 70 Other Ranks. Each shift was to have a minimum of 1 Officer and 7 men. Eventually, the men who had volunteered for such duties would receive special unit designations introduced for Coastal Artillery Batteries. For example, the emergency Coastal Battery at Bexhill-on-Sea, East Sussex, was given the designation '301 Coast Battery'. However, it is not known with any certainty when such insignia was finally introduced - one ex-Home Guard states that this was certainly not before middle to late 1943. The Home Guard Coastal Artillery units were finally stood down on September 11th 1944.

The anklets that were uniquely Home Guard. Issued in mid-brown grained chrome leather, they were commonly stained black by the wearer.

Detail of the inside of 'Battledress Blouse, Serge' to show the unit stamp of the 6th City of Glasgow Home Guard.

Left: Members of the 21st Sussex (Eastbourne) Battalion, Home Guard, training on a 6" Coastal Gun on the seafront at Eastbourne. (By kind permission of Eastbourne Central Library).

Our Home Guard, undergoing training at the emergency Coastal Battery on the promenade at Worthing, is wearing standard battledress as per his parent unit. He has the addition of extra equipment relevant to his duties, such as the leather loop belt for ignition cartridges. A metal firing rod can be seen hanging from the loop belt on his back. He has a standard military issue pair of prismatic binoculars.

EQUIPMENT LIST
- Field Service Cap
- Battledress Blouse, Serge
- Battledress Trousers, Serge
- Home Guard Patt. leather anklets
- Ammunition boots
- Military issue prismatic binoculars
- Leather loop belt and ignition cartridges
- Firing rod

In 1942, the activities of the Home Guard were extended to include a new type of weapon - a 3-inch Rocket Projector commonly referred to as the 'Z' Battery. The No.2 Mark 1 Rocket Projector could fire one or two 3" rockets. Four guide rails were used, two to a rocket on each launcher. Two men laid each rocket, one traversing on the left, the other elevating on the right. Each Battery retained Regular Gunners from the Royal Artillery to assist in training and maintaining standards.

The first Batteries manned by the Home Guard became operational in Kent and London. The 101st Kent Home Guard 'Z' Battery, for example, was formed on July 14th 1942. At this stage it was known as the 178 'Z' Battery, or by its men as the 'Gillingham Battery'. Recruiting for all anti-aircraft detachments was strong - at this stage of the war it was considered by many that this would be the only method by which, as a Home Guard, they would be able to 'have-a-go' at the enemy. In London, as an illustration, from June 1942 enrolment for anti-aircraft gunners was running at several thousand per month. From this number, men were drawn either for service on the standard 3.7" anti-aircraft guns or for the newer 'Z' Batteries. The Home Guard were expected to carry out a specified number of duties per month. The duty crews would be collected, or arrive, on site at about 8pm, and remain on duty until 05.45am. They would sleep in huts on site, be fed and watered and only man the launchers during the course of training, or upon sounding of the station alarm.

The armband worn by L/Cpl. Richard J. Lilley. He served in the 197/104 City of London Home Guard A.A. 'Z' Battery, until transferring to the Lincolnshire Home Guard, for work reasons, in August 1943. This armband was found with a quantity of his correspondence. In this the reader finds descriptions of the 'Z' Batteries in operation, and even an attempt to shoot down a V-1 flying bomb. The black bow and arrow, aimed upwards, became the familiar badge of the regular anti-aircraft command. Originally it was worn by General Sir Frederick Pile's Headquarters, but from 1942 had become used throughout the command. In 1943 all Air Defence Units, including those of the Home Guard, officially adopted it for their use. Interestingly, in 1943 Light Anti-Aircraft rocket and gun detachments were once again issued with armbands. The reason was that time might not allow gunners to don full uniforms in the course of an alert, and it was felt that an armband would help him conform to the Geneva Convention.

Left: Two members of the 101st Kent Home Guard 'Z' Battery prepare their launcher for action. As far as can be seen, these men are only wearing the Home Guard shoulder title on their Battledress. (By kind permission of the Kent Messenger).

The uniform in general was as for normal Home Guard units, and only differed in having its own particular insignia. This varied considerably between units, and in this case he is wearing a locally produced khaki drill armband bearing the Anti Aircraft Command flash and one rank stripe denoting in this case "Lance Bombardier". He is wearing a leather Jerkin No.2, as drawn from unit stores for this type of duty, and has a Royal Artillery white woven cord lanyard, though the jerkin obscures this from view. He is carrying a Kodak 'Haze Screen For Aerial Observation'. Special leather gloves were provided for handling the projectiles, but our Home Guard has decided to leave them off.

EQUIPMENT LIST
- Steel helmet Mk. 2
- Leather Jerkin No.2
- Battle Dress Trousers, Serge
- Home Guard Patt. leather anklets
- Ammunition boots
- Kodak Haze Screen
- Service Patt. respirator in Mk. VI bag
- Locally produced anti-aircraft armband

Left: N.C.O.s who were armed with Mk.2 or Mk.3 Sten Machine Carbines were, from 1943, often issued an alternative pouch for the stick magazines. Based on the standard 1937 Patt. basic ammunition pouch, they were constructed to fit on the 1903 belt. Again we have front and rear views, supported by details of the manufacturer's markings.

Above: As early as 1940 there had been a partial issue of the 1939 Patt. leather basic ammunition pouches for Browning Automatic Rifle gunners. These issues were made on the ratio of one per gun. Subsequently, numbers of these pouches were issued to men armed with the Thompson Sub Machine Gun. Here we have front and rear views, along with a view of the manufacturer's markings. Where, with time, there were shortages of the 1937 Patt. Sten pouch, see left, these original leather pouches were modified. The depth was increased to accommodate the Sten magazines - such a modification can clearly be seen on the front view.

This then, in terms of uniform and equipment, was the ultimate Home Guard. Gone were the hastily assembled bits and pieces of equipment and home made weaponry. Dressed in full khaki serge battledress, bearing shoulder titles and regimental insignia, as would have been standard from 1942, he is armed with a Patt. 14 Enfield .303 rifle, and has the full equipment.

This is a composite design worn only by the Home Guard. It was based on the 1903 waist belt, and had a small pair of webbing ammunition pouches. Just as unique, and now very hard to find, was the 'sleeve, belt, web, Home Guard Pattern'. All this was joined by a pair of 1937 Patt. shoulder braces, a water bottle, and the haversack modified by the wearer to be worn as a small backpack.

In this example, the Home Guard can also be seen wearing his service respirator at the ready, his Mark 2 steel helmet, and a pair of ammunition boots. His Field Service Cap, (not shown), would bear the badge of The Duke of Wellington's West Riding Regiment.

By this stage in the war, the traditional 'Dad's Army' image of the Home Guard - a poorly equipped mixture of WW1 veterans and partly trained volunteers - had all but disappeared. The Home Guard was now a well disciplined and well armed body of men, with an average age of about 30. Trained by regular army instructors, they were not complacently sitting back and discounting the threat of invasion, which was still theoretically present. Most importantly, they still retained the Home Guard spirit and readiness to fight if the tide of war should turn once again.

EQUIPMENT LIST
- Mark 2 steel helmet
- Battledress Blouse, Serge
- Battledress Trousers, Serge
- 1937 Patt. webbing cross straps
- Service Patt. respirator and Mk. VI. bag
- Home Guard Patt. haversack
- 1903 Patt. waist belt
- Home Guard small ammunition pouches
- P.14 .303 Enfield rifle
- P.14 Enfield bayonet in 1939 Patt. frog
- Sleeve, belt, web, Home Guard Pattern
- Home Guard Patt. leather anklets
- Ammunition boots

An officer of the Wisborough Green, (West Sussex), Home Guard showing an unofficial item of insignia. On his chest can be seen a RAF half wing - possibly indicating the wearer's previous military service. (By kind permission of the Garland Collection and the West Sussex Records Office).

The blouse modelled here is the one worn by Lt. Col. T. Nickson, a World War One veteran late of the Kings Own Royal Lancaster Regiment. For the second time, in 1940, he acted in his Country's hour of need and enrolled in the L.D.V., ultimately achieving the rank of Major in the 4th Buckinghamshire Home Guard.

This unit's cap badge was that of The Oxford & Buckinghamshire Light Infantry, and their claim to fame was a self-appointed nickname of 'First Blood'. This title alluded to an incident at a roadblock involving a car full of soldiers returning late to their barracks. A refusal to stop prompted one of the Home Guard sentries to fire the mandatory shot at the disappearing car. The round passed through the rear window and accentuated the parting in the driver's hair. This is reputedly the first member of the regular British army to be shot by the Home Guard!

As did many officers in the Home Guard, he is wearing a leather 'Sam Browne' waist belt with a holster for his .455 Webley Mk.6 service revolver. If armed with a .380 service revolver he would probably be equipped with a 1937 Patt. webbing belt, holster and ammunition pouch. He is wearing 1937 Pattern webbing anklets and binocular case, a steel helmet and a service pattern respirator. If he had possessed them, he would be wearing brown leather private purchase officers boots, unlike in this example where he has on the standard O.R.s black ammunition boots. Officers usually had a khaki or olive green shirt with collar attached by studs, often worn with battledress blouse lapels open to show a tie. On certain occasions officers were allowed to wear service dress if they possessed it.

EQUIPMENT LIST
• Steel helmet Mark 2 • Battle Dress Blouse, Serge • Battle Dress Trousers, Serge • 1937 Patt. map case • Sam Browne belt and holster • 1937 Patt. webbing anklets • Webley Mark 6 .455 revolver • Service pattern respirator and Mk. VI. bag • 1937 Patt. binoculars and case • Ammunition boots

Detailed here is the blouse of a Platoon Commander of the 3rd Battalion, Aberdeen Kincardine, (Scotland), Home Guard. Here we can see all the insignia of late 1941 onwards, but still retaining the early blue stripe rank marking that was theoretically obsolete by this time.

Insignia detail of the blouse of a Major in the 4th Bucks Home Guard. Khaki worsted crowns as worn by the regular army are stitched to the shoulder straps of this blouse.

OFFICERS AND N.C.O.s RANK MARKINGS.

L.D.V. Appointment markings as set down in Army Council Instruction 653, dated June 24th 1940:

Zone Commander	4 dark blue cloth stripes on each shoulder strap.
Battalion Commander	3 on each shoulder strap.
Company Commander	2 on each shoulder strap.
Platoon Commander	1 on each shoulder strap.
Section Commander	3 worsted chevrons.

Home Guard rank markings as set down in Army Council Instruction 924, dated August 15th 1940:

Zone Commander	1 dark blue cloth stripe 2in. deep on each shoulder strap.
Group Commander	4 stripes 3/8in. deep on each shoulder
Battalion Commander	3 stripes 3/8in. deep on each shoulder.
Company Commander	2 stripes 3/8in. on each shoulder.
Platoon Commander	1 stripe 3/8in. on each shoulder.
Section Commander	3 worsted chevrons.
Squad Commander	2 worsted chevrons.

Home Guard rank badges as set down originally in War Office urgent postal telegram BM/1051/H.G.2(a), dated March 13th 1941. Was reprinted as Army Council Instruction 623 of April 24th 1941, and further clarified in Army Council Instruction 1273 of July 19th 1941:

Brigadier	Three stars set in a triangle and surmounted by a crown.
Colonel	Crown above two stars.
Lieutenant-Colonel	Crown above single star.
Major	Single crown.
Captain	Three stars in a row.
Lieutenant	Two stars in a row.
Second Lieutenant	Single star.
Warrant Officer Class I	Royal Arms in worsted.
Warrant Officer Class II	Crown set within wreath all in worsted.
Sergeant	Three worsted chevrons.
Corporal	Two worsted chevrons.
Lance Corporal	One worsted chevron.

Officers insignia on shoulder straps of blouses in worsted embroidery, or on the shoulder straps of greatcoats in gilt. Officers of the rank of Colonel and above, may wear scarlet gorget patches on the collars of the battledress as laid down for officers of corresponding rank in the Regular Army.

Here we can see one of 3,000 or so men, chosen for their superior knowledge of their own localities and the surrounding countryside, who were recruited into small secret units labelled on paper as Home Guard. With the express purpose of confusing the enemy, these were actually 'sabotage squads' that were even equipped with hidden bunkers.

The idea behind such units had been around for some time, particularly since the birth of Section 'D', which was formed as part of the Secret Intelligence Service in March 1938. It was not until May 1940, with the military situation in Europe rapidly deteriorating, that the Home Guard Auxiliary Units were formed. This tight-structured and extremely (even now) secretive resistance formation was instigated by, amongst others, one Colonel Colin Gubbins. Most of the men, though not all, were drawn from the ranks of existing Home Guard Units. All the men were required to sign the Official Secrets Act, and on joining the Auxiliary Units were immediately issued with a complete uniform bearing the number of their battalion. In all, there were three battalions: 201st, which covered Scotland; 202nd in the North of England; and the 203rd in Southern England. None of these battalions were given official recognition, and the title of Home Guard Auxiliaries was intended more to assist with maintaining a cover for their operations and protection if captured, than to indicate any actual link with the Home Guard proper.

Not even their own families knew what the members of the Auxiliary Battalions had been recruited to do. In the event of an invasion these specially trained men would go to ground, and commence their missions of attacking behind lines of communication and at vital strategic installations. It was intended that they would cause as much disruption and confusion as possible to the advancing enemy in an attempt to allow the Regular Army time to regroup and, hopefully, counter attack.

Our operative is one of the few Home Guardsmen to be given the last variation of wartime battle dress - the 1940, Utility, Pattern. This had buttons exposed and minimal pleating. Also, unusually for an Other Rank, he is wearing a 1937 Pattern webbing waist belt and anklets. He has been issued with a snipers camouflage printed face veil - a standard issue to many Home Guardsmen. Well armed, he carries a .45 calibre Thompson Sub Machine Gun; Fairbairn Sykes Mark 2 fighting knife; an automatic pistol in its leather holster, and a set of brass knuckle-dusters in his pocket. Around his body is a 6-foot toggle rope, which was also general issue to regular Home Guard units. This item has a multitude of uses, from making rope ladders and bridges, to forming towropes for heavy items of equipment such as 3" O.S.B. guns (the Smith Guns).

Within his secret base, (O.B., or Operational Base), he would have a wireless, a supply of explosives and other equipment with which to carry out his desperate task. His rations were to last about a fortnight, this being his expected maximum life expectancy behind what would, in effect, be enemy lines.

Set of brass knuckle-dusters as used by men of the Regular Special Forces and Auxiliary Battalions.

Metal studded, lead-bored, wooden club issued to Auxiliary Battalions. (By kind permission of Mr. S. Angell)

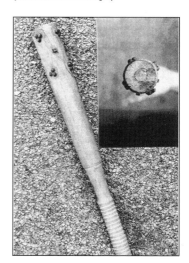

EQUIPMENT LIST:
- **Camouflage scrim scarf**
- **Battledress Blouse, 1940 Patt.**
- **Battledress Trousers, 1940 Patt.**
- **1937 Patt. waist belt and leather holster**
- **Toggle rope**
- **Thompson Sub Machine-Gun**
- **Fairbairn Sykes fighting knife Mark 2**
- **1937 Patt. webbing anklets**
- **Ammunition boots**

The medical services of the Home Guard were established later than most other branches that existed to serve the fighting man. It was Col. W.C. Harthill, Medical Advisor G.H.Q. Home Forces, who drafted the original scheme for a Home Guard Medical Service. This was discussed between the War Office, G.H.Q. Home Forces, Ministry of Health, Ministry of Home Security and the British Medical Association on April 2nd 1941. On this date, instructions were issued providing the basis of the organisation and the equipment required.

Indeed, Army Council Instruction 468, of April 2nd 1941, gives us a Medical Equipment issue scale for a platoon of approximately 100 men. It was as follows: 2 x stretchers; blankets, brown, 3 for each stretcher; 1 x outfit, first aid, large; 1 x haversacks, shell dressing; 1 x wooden splints, plain, sets; 2 x water bottles and carriers, ordnance pattern, 1 for each stretcher squad; 8 x brassards, 'S.B.', 4 for each stretcher squad; and 1 x brassard 'Red Cross', for each medical officer.

As with the Home Guard as a whole, the Medical Branch underwent constant changes and transformations. A fact finding mission took place in early 1942, the result of which was Army Council Instruction 780, dated April 13th 1942. This was considered to be the Home Guard 'bible' on the provision of medical services. It clarified the matter that the Home Guard was intended to care for casualties up to the point of transport to, and treatment at, a hospital. From this point on, the casualty was to come under the care of the civilian Civil Defence Authorities. To achieve this A.C.I. 780 formulated a scheme of Casualty Collecting Posts, (C.C.P.s), operating at platoon level. Through these, the casualties would be passed over to the Civil Defence Casualty Organisation.

Each Home Guard Battalion formed its own medical organisation, based upon the Army Council Instructions. In the Suffolk Home Guard, for example, each Battalion had three Medical Officers and one Medical Sergeant. Each platoon had a Medical Corporal assisted by a deputy (a Private, such as the stretcher-bearer illustrated here). The standard required of the Medical Corporals in first aid, was that of the St. John's Ambulance Certificate.

Our man is wearing standard serge battledress with a Red Cross armband. Officially these were intended for medical officers only, but came to be worn by bearers when 'S.B.' (stretcher-bearer) armbands were not available. He has a webbing haversack containing shell dressings, and is holding a standard pattern military stretcher. His respirator is at the slung position and his steel helmet is carried on his left shoulder in the regulation position.

After assisting the Home Guard unofficially since the very beginning, the government finally recognised the ladies' contribution to the movement. On April 20th 1943 it was announced that a limited number of women would be accepted, or as they termed it 'nominated', for a number of specific duties. These tasks included driving, telephone operating, cooking and assorted clerical duties.

The plastic wartime 'economy' lapel badge of the Home Guard Women's Auxiliary sections. These were issued in 1943 and 1944. This example was manufactured by A. Stanley & Sons, Walsall.

Originally it had been felt that women were too useful in the Civil Defence organisations, so whilst allowing entry, of sorts, into the Home Guard, they could not be provided with uniforms, considering the difficulties met in fitting out the Home Guard proper. Ultimately, the only mark of their affiliation with the organisation was an officially sanctioned plastic lapel badge. This plastic, gold coloured badge, bearing the letters 'HG' was to be pinned on the left side of their outer clothing.

In many units, female volunteers had been in 'service' for some time. One of the earliest cases, if not the first, could be that of the A2 'Shore' Company, Upper Thames Patrol, L.D.V. On August 29th 1940 a meeting was held, at Wallingford in Surrey, where over 40 Female Volunteers were recruited. To quote the unit Commander, "we blissfully ignored the rules concerning women in the Home Guard". These female volunteers were used predominately as drivers, and were even supplied with their own uniform. The Upper Thames Patrol is also known to have issued some of their female members with black caps bearing the U.T.P. badge and armbands with the inscription 'U.T.P.'.

Other units provided their own quasi-military uniforms for their Female Auxiliaries. The Air Ministry Auxiliary Section, for example, turned out their ladies in navy blue boiler suits, matching side cap and arm bands embroidered 'AMAS'. Other units had varying khaki composite ensembles of service clothing, but particularly Field Service Caps and skirts.

The Auxiliary shown here is wearing a typical ladies suit of the period. Along with the plastic pin-back lapel badge, she is carrying her civilian issue gas mask in a fabric shoulder bag.

Private, 2nd Hampshire (Whitchurch) Battalion Home Guard. 1940.

The subject is wearing the unique Home Guard cape first issued in the summer of 1940. These were an interim measure, introduced as a result of the shortage of Greatcoats. They carried on in service side by side with those Greatcoats that had been issued, until supplies of the latter allowed standardisation.

CAPES, SERGE
HOME GUARD.

SIZE **SMALL.**
Height, 5/4 — 5/6
Breast, 37 — 39

JAMES S. TRIBE, LTD.
— 1940 —

Right: Detail of the label in the Home Guard cape.

Private, 33rd Surrey (County Borough of Croydon) Battalion Home Guard. 1941.

This Home Guard has now received his Greatcoat, Dismounted, 1940 Pattern.

GREAT COAT DISMOUNTED
1940 Pattern

SIZE **II**

HEIGHT 6/1 — 6/2
BREAST 41 — 43

THE REGO CLOTHIERS LTD.
January 1942

This was also worn by the Regular Army, and was a vital piece of equipment to any man destined to spend long nights on cold and exposed hill or cliff top sentry duty.

Inset: Detail of manufacturer's label in a 1940 Patt. Greatcoat.

Rear view of 1940 Patt. Greatcoat when worn.

Southern Railway Home Guards on an exercise at Gillingham, August 2nd 1941. The Home Guard on the right is, unlike the others, wearing a gas cape. Gas Protection capes were worn as a foul weather garment when nothing else was available.

However, Home Guard Information Circular No.5 of November 8th 1941 stated: "Anti-gas capes are now being issued to the Home Guard. These capes lose their protective quality rapidly when exposed to wind and weather. They should, therefore, only be worn when necessary for operational reasons or training." (By kind permission of the Kent Messenger).

Sergeant, 3rd West Riding Battalion Home Guard. Late 1943.

This volunteer is wearing his rubberised Groundsheet Cape Mk.VIII as issued to the Regular Army. This was an interim stopgap, and when stocks of Greatcoats permitted, these were completely withdrawn from issue.

Below: Detail of a manufacturer's stamp on a Groundsheet Cape Mk. VIII.

Above: A member of the Rustington, West Sussex, Home Guard, in a hide showing how a Field Service Cap may be worn with the sides folded down. (By kind permission of Mrs M. Taylor).

Universal Pattern Field Service Cap, khaki drab gabardine with 2 small general service buttons. It was originally issued to the L.D.V. without cap badge. The British Army originally adopted this type of headgear in 1893, and it has gone in and out of fashion periodically ever since.

Universal Pattern Field Service Cap with badge of the Hampshire Regiment - as worn by most Hampshire Home Guard units. Regimental badges were authorised to be worn on August 3rd 1940.

Universal Pattern Field Service Cap of the 3rd Aberdeen and Kincardine Battalion Home Guard circa 1941. The Scottish Home Guard units were unique in wearing

bonnet badges on side caps. In time, national pride took over, and side caps were replaced as soon as possible with the Tam O Shanter.

Above: A Tam O Shanter, bearing the badge of the Argyll and Sutherland Highlanders, as would have been worn by the Argyllshire Home Guard circa 1944. At this stage of the war the Tam O Shanter had replaced the Field Service Cap in Scottish Home Guard units.

Detail of the lining of the Tam O Shanter, with the manufacturer's marking.

Detail of the lining of the Tam O Shanter showing the War Office markings and WD stamp.

Below: A pair of Mark II Respirator Spectacles in their original protective case. These became standard issue to certain members of the Home Guard. Army Council Instruction 1669, dated September 4th 1941, stated that one pair of Mark III (War Office Pattern) respirator spectacles and case will be supplied, at the public expense, to members of the Home Guard who normally require spectacles to enable them to shoot accurately.

Officers khaki Service Dress Cap, bearing the badge of The Royal West Kent Regiment, as worn by many of the Kent Home Guard battalions. This item of headgear was not officially sanctioned, but still worn by some officers and provided at their own expense.

Serge Service Dress Cap, Other Ranks. These were most likely to be seen being worn by those Home Guard serving in the mounted units. Cadet units absorbed by the Home Guard also wore them.

Above: A Mark II British Steel Helmet. For many units, the issue, or rather lack of issue, of such equipment was a cause for concern for some time. Eventually, every Home Guard would eventually have one in his possession. Below: On the left is an inside view of a Mark 1. Steel Helmet, (with pad), and on the right, a Mark 2. Steel Helmet, (no pad).

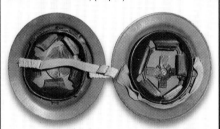

One example not illustrated here is the crash helmet issued to motorcycle despatch riders. Army Council Instruction 2502, dated December 15th 1941, formally gave permission for the Home Guard to be issued such items alongside protective clothing. In the supporting correspondence to the T.A. Associations, reference 54/H.G./97(T.A.(2)), it was stressed that any issue would be on the basis of operational priority.

Right: The two main types of headgear as issued to the Home Guard - both being sported by members of the 20th Sussex (Hailsham) Battalion, Home Guard. The first is the Mark II Steel Helmet. This is being worn by Cpl. P.E. Midnore, the Champion Shot of East Sussex, 1944. The second, is a picture of Lt. C.W. Gibbs. Wearing the Field Service Cap, Gibbs was the Champion Battalion Shot of both 1942 and 1943. (Kind permission of the Sussex Archeological Society).

Army Council Instructions also provide a list of personal items of anti-gas equipment, that were eventually issued to all Home Guardsmen. This reads thus:
Respirator, (complete).
Cape, Anti-Gas No.1. (When not available, Capes, Groundsheet Mk.8. were allowed as a substitute).
Ointment, A.G. (2-oz. containers).
Eyeshields, A.G. (packet of 6).
Wallets, Anti-Gas. No.1.
Cotton Waste.

Left: As ever with the Home Guard, there were exceptions to the rules. Some units employed their own, and often unique, forms of headgear. The Upper Thames Patrol (U.T.P.) for example, were officially permitted to wear black peaked caps with a distinctive U.T.P. badge - an example of which can be seen here.

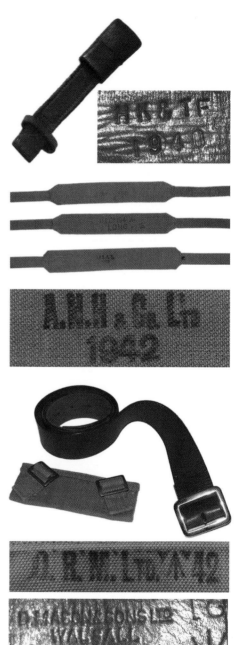

Above: Men of the 21st Sussex (Eastbourne) Battalion, Home Guard on exercise.

In this rear view we can see how the equipment of the average Home Guard in 1943 and 1944 might look. (By kind permission of Eastbourne Central Library).

Equipment shown on this page (from top to bottom):

- Leather 1939 Patt. bayonet frog.

- Markings on the 1939 Patt. leather bayonet frog.

- Pair of 1937 Patt. webbing cross-straps.

- 1937 Patt. rubberised cross-strap.

- Markings on rubberised cloth, (webbing substitute), type 1937 Patt. cross-strap, as used by the Home Guard.

- 1903 Patt. leather waist belt.

- Front view of the sleeve, belt, web, Home Guard Patt.

- Markings on the sleeve, belt, web, Home Guard Patt.

- Close up of 1903 Patt. leather waist belt manufacturer's markings.

(Kind permission of
the Sussex
Archeological Society)

Above: Home Guard rubberised fabric haversack with close up of markings on inside of flap.

Below: Webbing ammunition pouch with internal view showing markings.

The ultimate Home Guard! Here a member of the 20th Sussex (Hailsham) Battalion Home Guard stands on guard.

Below: Mk. IV water bottle and leather cradle with close up of markings.

To end with, we have created a small display of items of uniform used in the filming of the hit television series 'Dad's Army'. It is this comedy series, first screened by the BBC over the years 1968-77, which has done so much to retain the Home Guard in the nation's memory. Starring the likes of Arthur Lowe, John Le Mesurier and Clive Dunn, amongst others, it has proven to be so untiringly popular and well loved that hardly a week goes by without an episode being repeated on the BBC or other channel. All the items shown here are from the author's private collection, and were all sourced from theatrical costumiers who were known to have worked with the BBC on the sets of 'Dad's Army'.

Interestingly, the items on the page will help illustrate just how much 'artistic licence' the production teams used. For example, the Denim Overall Blouse worn by Arthur Lowe as Captain George Mainwaring - the C.O. of the Walmington-on-Sea Platoon - in series one and two, has nothing whatsoever to do with the Second World War. This can be seen in the middle of the picture. It is, in fact, a National Service period blouse dated 1955. Although his rank markings have since been removed, the stitching of Mainwaring's Captain's pips can still be clearly seen.

Also in the collection, are original first pattern serge battledress blouses, worn by two members of the 'Walmington-on-Sea Platoon' - Michael Moore and Freddie Wiles. Although now denuded of their famous, and completely fictional 'CP 1' county designation insignia, they still bear the wardrobe nametags in the linings. Moore and Wiles clocked up nearly 60 episodes apiece in their role as non-speaking members of the platoon. It is worth pointing out that the CP designation does not stand for Cinque Ports as many believe. It is in fact derived from the surnames of the inventors of 'Dad's Army' - David Croft and Jimmy Perry.

Finally, whilst we are on the showbiz Home Guard tack, we should not forget the supportive contributions of that much loved entertainer George Formby. His songs about the Home Guard, and patriotic comedy film 'Get Cracking', betray the very warm feelings that he felt towards the original Home Guard.

Right: The name 'A. Lowe' as marked by a member of the wardrobe staff. As in the regular army, names were written in an actor's uniform to prevent confusion and therefore save time. After all, even on a film set, one piece of battledress looks remarkably like any other!

Right: The Field Service Cap of John Le Mesurier. He wore this, as Sergeant Arthur Wilson, in the earlier TV series and in the motion picture 'Dad's Army', which was released in 1971. It is a theatrically produced 'prop', made of First World War type serge material. Later he would wear original military Field Service Caps. Inside, we can see the name 'Le Mesurier' as marked, once again, by wardrobe staff.